YOU K
GETTING

Emo

SUMMERSDALE

Summersdale Publishers Ltd
46 West Street
Chichester
PO19 1RP

www.summersdale.com

ISBN 1 84024 197 7

Printed and bound in Great Britain

Text by Emma Burgess
Cartoons by Kate Taylor

You know you're getting old when . . .

YOU KNOW YOU'RE GETTING OLD WHEN . . .

Every sentence starts with
'In my day...'

You drink too much...tea.

YOU KNOW YOU'RE GETTING OLD WHEN . . .

Your idea of a sporty weekend is spent on the Bowling Green.

You don't bother to re-decorate your house because your kids are already making plans to convert it into flats once you're gone.

9

Life begins at 50.
Make that 60.

You think the Internet is
something fishermen use.

YOU KNOW YOU'RE GETTING OLD WHEN . . .

You try and talk into your TV's remote control.

You constantly complain that sitcoms aren't funny any more. You remember The Coronation. Wasn't George VI dashing?

Your partner leaves you.
Well, death is inevitable.

You are very sociable. Well, there's a funeral a week at the moment.

You think the sex scenes in the Bond films are pornographic.

You're so hot in bed. Aren't electric blankets great?

You just can't understand
why racism is offensive.

You're desperate to find a suitable religion that will ensure a good return on your investment.

You have developed a taste
for tinned pilchards.

YOU KNOW YOU'RE GETTING OLD WHEN . . .

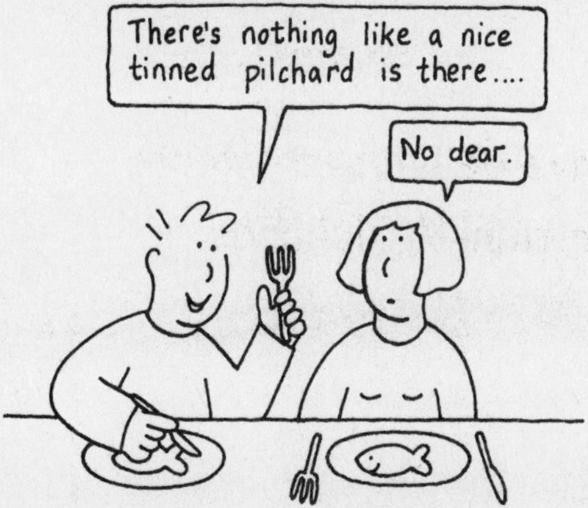

YOU KNOW YOU'RE GETTING OLD WHEN . . .

You have just opened a
subscription to
Reader's Digest.

You spend a lot of time pottering in your shed...even though you have no garden.

YOU KNOW YOU'RE GETTING OLD WHEN . . .

Your family subtly tries to ascertain what sort of send off you'd like.

You think your new, totally nondescript jacket is really snazzy.

YOU KNOW YOU'RE GETTING OLD WHEN . . .

Your slippers are more worn down than your shoes.

YOU KNOW YOU'RE GETTING OLD WHEN . . .

You think a 'mobile' is a phone on wheels.

Your 'rosebuds' – as your
husband used to call them –
are now more like
hanging baskets.

You cancel your subscription to *What Car?* and replace it with one for *What Wheelchair?*

YOU KNOW YOU'RE GETTING OLD WHEN . . .

Even golf wears you out.

You would record *Songs of Praise*...if only you could work the video.

You grumble about how nice the old-style British passports were – even though you've never left the country.

You still refer to the EU as the EEC, and can't see how it fits into the British Empire.

You would definitely fail
your driving test if you had
to take it these days. Cars
have engines now for a
start.

The mention of KY Jelly no longer makes you laugh.

You keep abreast of latest fashions by popping into your local branch of *Past Times* every now and then.

Your choice of shoe wear is
determined by what your
doctor prescribes for you...

...come to think of it, so is
your choice of underwear.

You have more plastic in your hips than in your wallet.

47

You are not worried about
losing the Pound to the
Euro...you're still busy trying
to cope with decimalisation.

You consider buying a sports car for weekends – a *Reliant Robin* would be perfect.

YOU KNOW YOU'RE GETTING OLD WHEN . . .

You get asked your age
on the bus.

You are still collecting
Green Shield Stamps. Bless.

YOU KNOW YOU'RE GETTING OLD WHEN . . .

You wear a hat, scarf and full-length coat to keep out that August chill.

Going bald is no longer a
worry for you...your
husband's losing his eyesight
at last.

You think that modern air travel isn't safe enough. I mean, just look at the *Hindenberg*.

Your application for *Blind Date* is turned down – they don't do the one for oldies any more.

The specs you wear are
thicker than glass bricks.

You can recite the ingredients of every anti-wrinkle cream on the market.

YOU KNOW YOU'RE GETTING OLD WHEN . . .

59

YOU KNOW YOU'RE GETTING OLD WHEN . . .

You have so many age spots, your grandchildren regularly play 'join the dots'...to find they make an old person.

You panic when friends threaten to organise a birthday party for you...because your lungs failed the last time you tried to blow out all those candles.

You still enjoy sport, but you've swapped your weights for a pair of knitting needles.

Your idea of being
irresponsible is spending
your weekly pension on
something other than food
and heating.

You recall your happy
teenage memories in black
and white.

YOU KNOW YOU'RE GETTING OLD WHEN . . .

Your baby pictures are in sepia.

You think that buying stuff 'online' is exclusive to trapeze artists.

You are saving up for
Cryogenic Preservation.

YOU KNOW YOU'RE GETTING OLD WHEN . . .

Policemen seem younger than your kids.

YOU KNOW YOU'RE GETTING OLD WHEN . . .

The smutty jokes you used to tell now appear on Kiddies TV.

You're a regular on shows like *Trisha* and *Kilroy* – along with the rest of the bus load from the Old People's Home.

Your home videos are
shot in cine-film.

You think Alan
Titchmarsh is sexy.

Anyone with hair
seems young.

Beige contains all the
spectrums of your rainbow.

YOU KNOW YOU'RE GETTING OLD WHEN . . .

Sex with you is classed as necrophilia.

YOU KNOW YOU'RE GETTING OLD WHEN . . .

Your nipples smudge the varnish on your toenails.

YOU KNOW YOU'RE GETTING OLD WHEN . . .

You remember the days when *Coca Cola* still contained cocaine.

And Opium was something you inhaled, not splashed behind your ears.

80

You don't need to visit your dentist anymore...you just send him your teeth in the post.

You've forgotten the Language of Love, but you're fluent in Bingo Lingo.

YOU KNOW YOU'RE GETTING OLD WHEN . . .

You are ready to
retire...from
retirement itself.

You audition as the Thora Hird replacement in the chair lift ads, but are rejected because you're too old.

YOU KNOW YOU'RE GETTING OLD WHEN . . .

Your hair comes out of a can.

YOU KNOW YOU'RE GETTING OLD WHEN . . .

You're no longer into politics.
Not since your favourite MP
- Mr Gladstone - retired.

You wonder what all the fuss with obsessive dieting is about. You keep your figure trim with the aid of a corset and crinoline.

You refuse to give into this *PlayStation* lark...until they bring out *Lara Croft plays Hoop and Stick.*

You think that the problem of transport pollution could be eased by shoveling up all the horse dung.

Your idea of Modern Art is
cave drawings.

You think satellite TV is something that only the crew of Apollo 13 could receive.

You refuse to believe that woman have the Vote.

YOU KNOW YOU'RE GETTING OLD WHEN . . .

You start to reminisce about major incidents in your youth. The Boer War affects you to this day.

You've not yet mastered modern plumbing. Those tin baths in front of the fire are a bind.

You can't see the point of
flushing toilets. It's just as
easy to tip your bed-pan out
of the window.

You no longer apologise for farting...actually, you don't even notice.

Your kids are going
bald and grey.

YOU KNOW YOU'RE GETTING OLD WHEN . . .

YOU KNOW YOU'RE GETTING OLD WHEN . . .

You have a sticker in the back of your car that reads 'My other one's a horse and cart'.

YOU KNOW YOU'RE GETTING OLD WHEN . . .

You start keeping budgerigars...and actually enjoying their company.

Your idea of a great Friday
night is a jug of mead at the
local tavern.

Your panic if you miss your winter flu-jab.

You're convinced that The
Talkies won't catch on.

YOU KNOW YOU'RE GETTING OLD WHEN . . .

When people hear you
muttering under your breath
about 'kids today' they don't
realise you're talking about
40 year olds.

Funeral directors try to
befriend you.

Your friends admire you because you still have a full set of teeth...they're not to know you keep them in a drawer.

Your idea of extravagant is having your Will translated into several different languages.

You give up smoking to save money... *Woodbines* aren't cheap, you know.

Your children are planning
their retirement parties.

You're not aware that your car has more than one gear. 1st seems to get you everywhere you want to go.

You are shocked when your
children talk about being
stoned. That's a pretty
barbaric hobby to
have, surely?

You join a choral group...even though you can't sing.

You have a very impressive
collection of disposable
plastic bags, which you
lovingly fold away and keep.

The only exciting post you are likely to receive these days is a post-mortem.

You don't buy bunches of flowers anymore, just wreaths. It's good to be prepared.

A car alarm in the street
goes off and you rush to the
nearest air-raid shelter.

YOU KNOW YOU'RE GETTING OLD WHEN . . .

You start advertising for
your own pallbearers.

You take up DIY. Well, if you could make your own coffin that would save on death duties.

You have terrible dry rot...
you really ought to
see the doctor.

You stop on the motorway hard shoulder...to admire the view.

You keep your First World War service pistol in case you're called up again.

The only letters you have
after your name are HRT.

You have trouble parking
your *Rover Metro*.

Your wardrobe is a
sea of beige.

**For the latest humour books
from Summersdale, check out**

www.summersdale.com